KU-662-105

Fantasy Field Trips

A Journey to the Centre of the Earth

Claire Throp

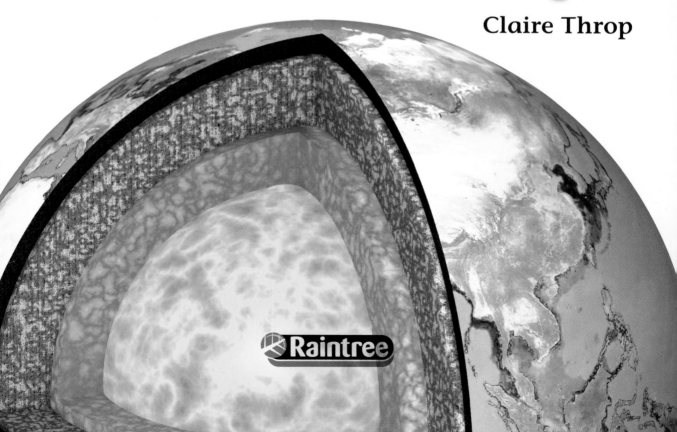

Raintree

Raintree is an imprint of Capstone Global Library Limited, a company incorporated in England and Wales having its registered office at 7 Pilgrim Street, London, EC4V 6LB – Registered company number: 6695582

www.raintreepublishers.co.uk
myorders@raintreepublishers.co.uk

Text © Capstone Global Library Limited 2014
First published in hardback in 2014
The moral rights of the proprietor have been asserted.

All rights reserved. No part of this publication may be reproduced in any form or by any means (including photocopying or storing it in any medium by electronic means and whether or not transiently or incidentally to some other use of this publication) without the written permission of the copyright owner, except in accordance with the provisions of the Copyright, Designs and Patents Act 1988 or under the terms of a licence issued by the Copyright Licensing Agency, Saffron House, 6–10 Kirby Street, London EC1N 8TS (www.cla.co.uk). Applications for the copyright owner's written permission should be addressed to the publisher.

Edited by Dan Nunn and Catherine Veitch
Designed by Cynthia Akiyoshi
Picture research by Ruth Blair
Production by Vicki Fitzgerald
Originated by Capstone Global Library Limited
Printed and bound in China

ISBN 978 1 406 27184 3
17 16 15 14 13
10 9 8 7 6 5 4 3 2 1

British Library Cataloguing in Publication Data
A full catalogue record for this book is available from the British Library.

Acknowledgements
We would like to thank the following for permission to reproduce photographs: Alamy pp. 14 (© Thomas R. Fletcher), 20 (© GC Minerals), 27 (© Inga Spence); Corbis pp. 13 (© KYODO/Reuters), 26 (© Rob Howard); Shutterstock pp. 4 (© Miks), 7 (© Kenneth Keifer), 10 (© Justin Atkins), 17 (© Serg Zastavkin), 18 (© clearviewstock), 21 (© Mopic), 22 and title page (© Lukiyanova Natalia/frenta); Superstock pp. 5 (Boomer Jerritt/All Canada Photos), 6, 12 (dieKleinert), 9 (Robert Harding Picture Library), 8 (Ragnar Th. Sigurdsson/age fotostock), 11 (Flirt), 15 (TAO Images), 16 (Jason Friend/Loop Images), 19 (Jim Sugar/Science Faction), 23 (Tips Images), 24, 29 (imagebroker.net), 25 (John Cancalosi/age fotostock), 28 (Clover).

Cover photograph of the caves of Sarawak, Borneo, Malaysia, reproduced with permission of Shutterstock (© gualtiero boffi).

Every effort has been made to contact copyright holders of material reproduced in this book. Any omissions will be rectified in subsequent printings if notice is given to the publisher.

All the Internet addresses (URLs) given in this book were valid at the time of going to press. However, due to the dynamic nature of the Internet, some addresses may have changed, or sites may have changed or ceased to exist since publication. While the author and publisher regret any inconvenience this may cause readers, no responsibility for any such changes can be accepted by either the author or the publisher.

GREENWICH LIBRARIES	
BL	
3 8028 02153984 3	
Askews & Holts	30-Jul-2014
C551.1	£12.99
4373221	

Some words are shown in bold, **like this**. You can find out what they mean by looking in the glossary.

Contents

Let's take a trip through Earth!

You might think Earth is all about green fields, rows of houses, or skyscrapers. This trip is going to change your mind! We are going on a journey of exploration into the centre of Earth.

This cave is a good place to start drilling to the centre of Earth.

Earth's layers

First of all, we need to find out what to expect as we travel through Earth towards the **core**. Earth is a **globe** made up of three main layers: **crust**, **mantle** and core.

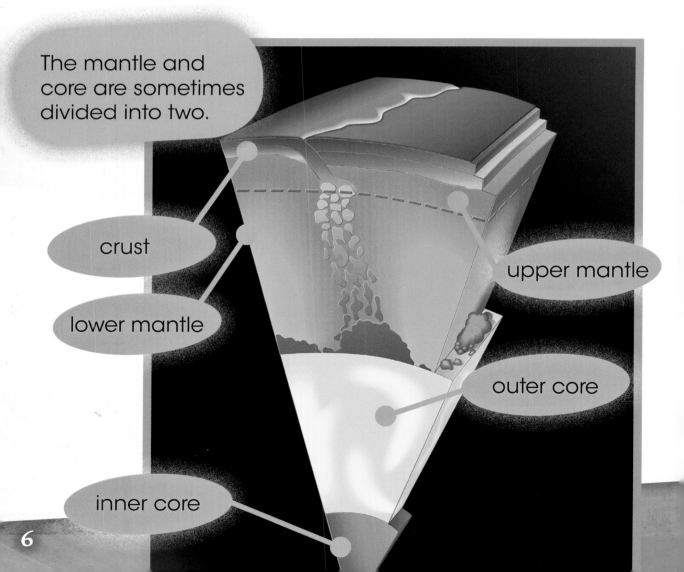

The mantle and core are sometimes divided into two.

crust

lower mantle

upper mantle

outer core

inner core

Jets of steaming water called **geysers** shoot up from inside Earth. They show how hot it is inside Earth.

The **crust** is the part of Earth we live on. The **mantle** is the next layer. The outer **core** is hot liquid and the inner core is an extremely hot solid.

Did you know?

Cracks in Earth's crust are called **fault lines**. The Mid-Atlantic Ridge in the Atlantic Ocean is a fault line.

Earthquakes happen along cracks in Earth's crust.

Crust

Earth's **crust** is made of solid rock. The crust is thickest under mountains and thinnest under oceans.

mountains

It may be a good idea to start drilling under the ocean, where the crust is thinnest.

Earth's **crust** is broken into several large pieces of rock and lots of smaller pieces. These pieces move a few centimetres each year. The pieces meeting or pulling apart can change the land we live on.

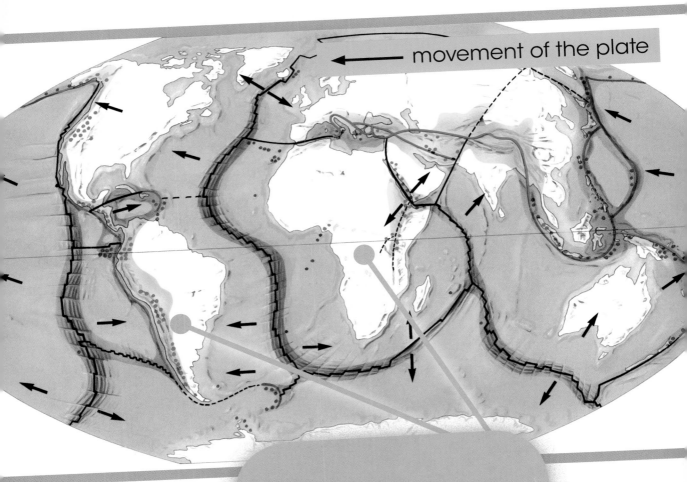

movement of the plate

The pieces of crust are called **tectonic plates**.

Drilling through Earth's crust will be difficult, but a powerful drill like this one should work.

13

Drilling through the crust

Deciding where to drill is difficult. Many mountains are made of **metamorphic rock**. Metamorphic rock is pushed up where pieces of Earth's **crust** meet. This rock is very hard and would not be easy to drill through.

metamorphic rock

Did you know?

The Himalayas
were made from
metamorphic rock
that was once at
the bottom of the
ocean. This means
it is possible to find
seashells at the top
of the mountains!

Most of Earth's **crust** is made up of **igneous rock**. The crust under the ocean may be thinner, but we would have to drill underwater. Let's drill through the crust under land.

This igneous rock is called dolerite.

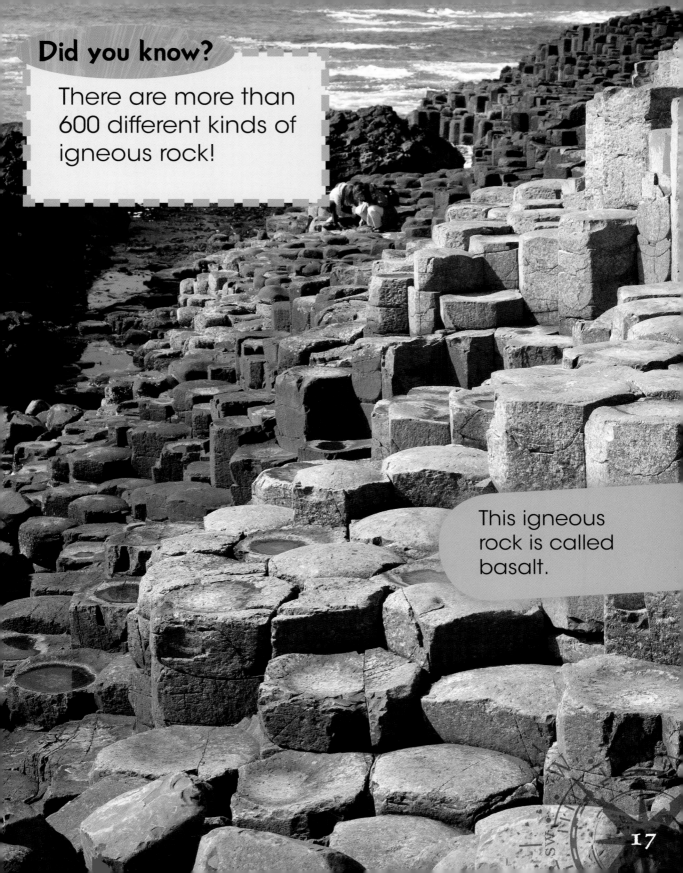

There are more than 600 different kinds of igneous rock!

This igneous rock is called basalt.

Upper mantle

We've made it through the **crust** and reached the upper **mantle**. It is getting hot in here! The upper mantle is made of liquid rock. The rock is so hot that it flows very slowly, like syrup.

When hot liquid rock bursts above ground, it is called **lava**.

Did you know?

The mantle is hot – it can reach temperatures of 3,700 degrees Celsius!

volcano

lava

Lava sometimes **erupts** out of volcanoes.

Lower mantle

Next, we drill to the lower **mantle**. This is made of solid rock. It includes **minerals** such as perovskite. Hold on tight, we are about to enter the **core**!

perovskite

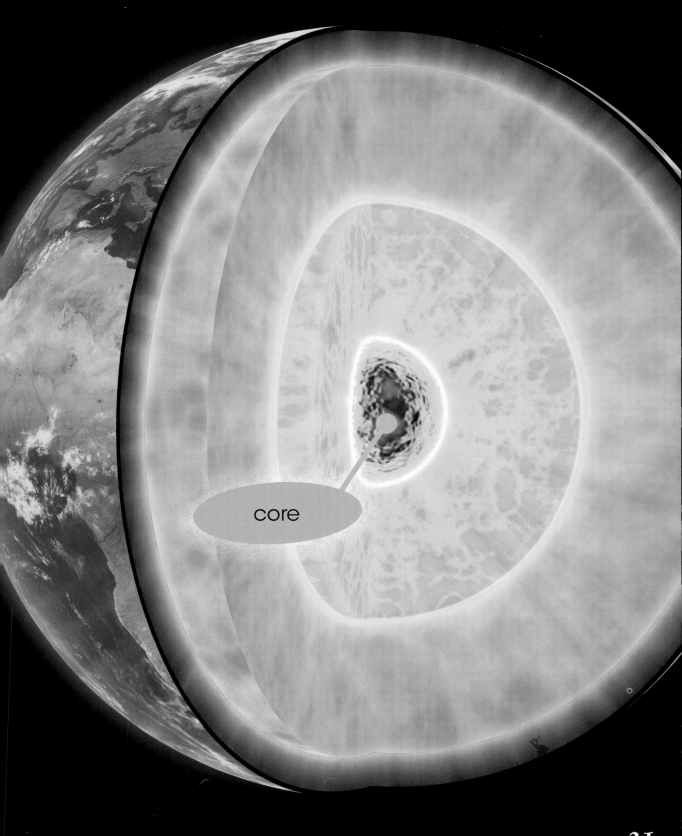

core

Outer core

Phew, it is really hot in here now! The outer **core** is made of liquid iron and nickel. Iron and nickel are both metals. The temperature in the outer core reaches 4,000 to 5,000 degrees Celsius.

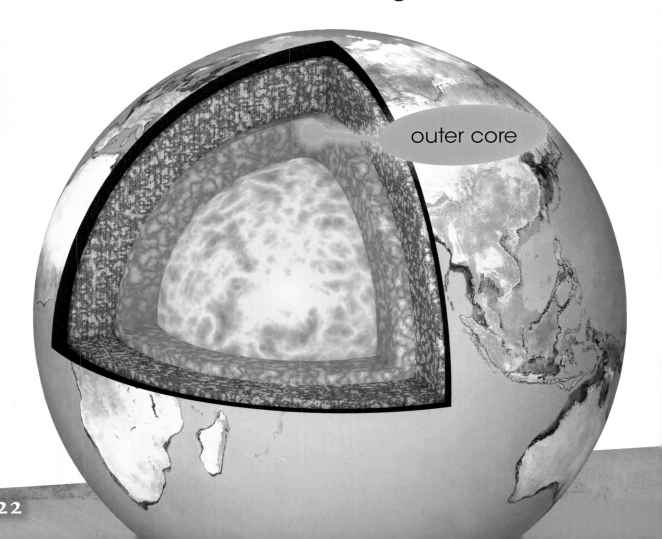

outer core

The outer core would look something like this extremely hot, melted iron.

Inner core

We've made it to the centre of Earth! The inner **core** of Earth is made mainly of the metals iron and some nickel. The temperature is thought to be between 5,000 and 7,000 degrees Celsius!

You may need a towel and some water!

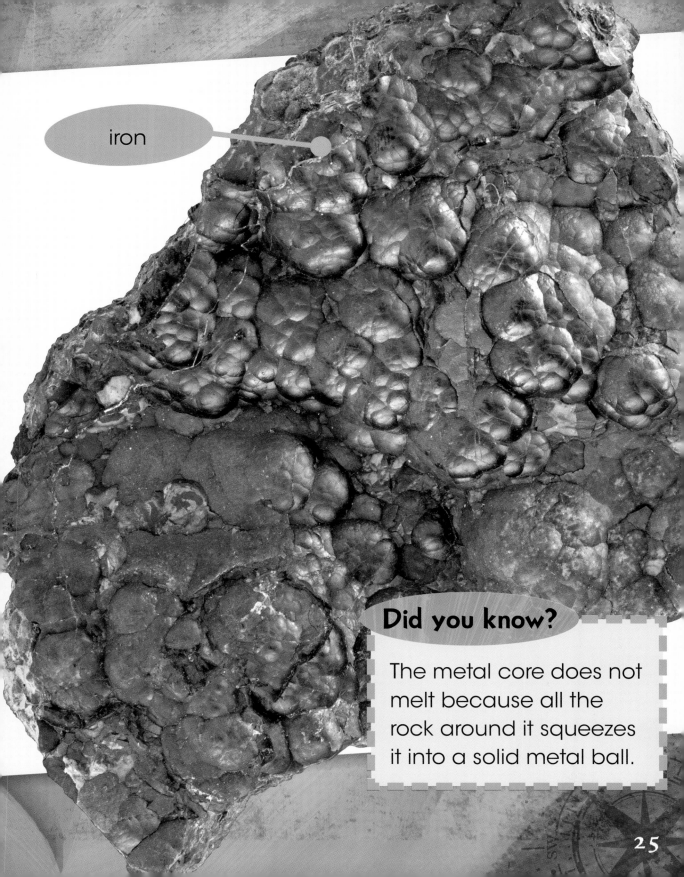

iron

Did you know?

The metal core does not melt because all the rock around it squeezes it into a solid metal ball.

How do we know?

Of course, it is not yet possible for us to really explore deep inside Earth. Scientists have discovered other ways of working out what goes on by studying earthquakes and rocks.

This scientist is studying a rock.

This machine measures the power of an earthquake.

Amazing Earth

That's the end of our journey. It is time to zoom back up to Earth's **crust** and head home.

What happens deep inside Earth affects the part of Earth we see. From rocks to volcanoes, from oceans to mountains, it's all connected to what goes on way below our feet.

This is what Earth looks like from space.

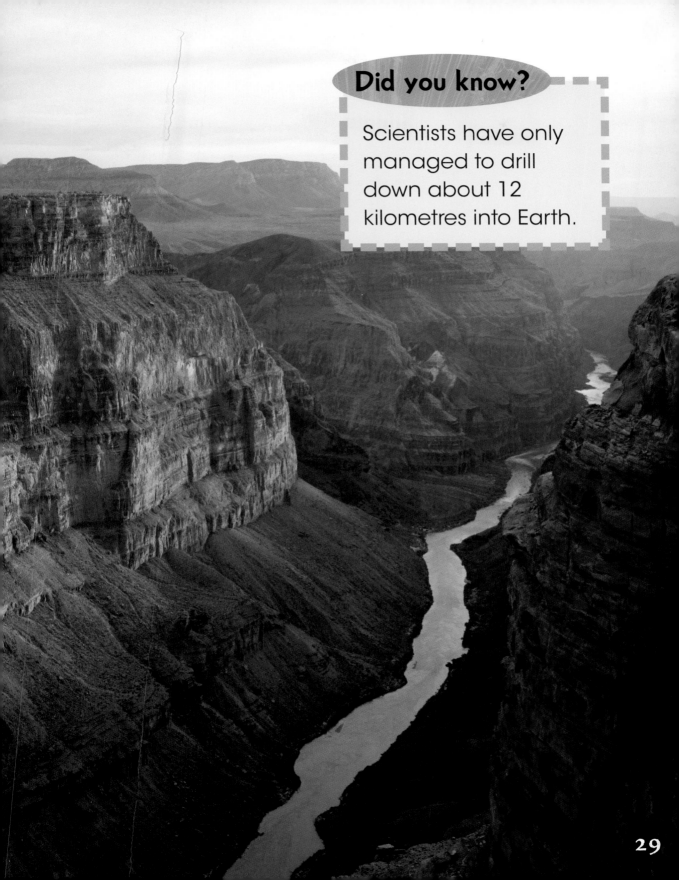

Did you know?

Scientists have only managed to drill down about 12 kilometres into Earth.

Glossary

core Earth's centre

crust outer layer of a planet

erupt push out lava and gases from under ground

fault line crack in Earth's crust

geyser jet of steaming water that shoots up from inside Earth

globe round object like a ball

igneous rock hot, melted rock

lava hot, melted rock above ground

mantle middle layer of Earth

metamorphic rock when great pressure or heat squeezes rock and changes it over time

mineral solid substance, such as gold or quartz, that can be found in the ground

tectonic plate one of a number of large pieces of rock that make up the outer surface of Earth

Find out more

Books

Earth, Elaine Landau (Children's Press, 2008)

Inside Earth (Earth Explorer), David Orme and
  Helen Orme (QED, 2011)

Volcano Explorers (Landform Adventurers),
  Pam Rosenberg (Raintree, 2011)

Volcanoes! (Eyewitness: Disaster), Helen Dwyer
  (Franklin Watts, 2011)

Websites

www.oum.ox.ac.uk/thezone/rocks/index.htm
  Discover more about the rock cycle on this website.

www.sciencekids.co.nz/sciencefacts/earth.html
  Find out more about Earth, including the different
  types of rock.

Index